My hair is
soft and smooth.

My hair is
big and soft!

My hair is
neat and textured!

This book belongs to

Acknowledgments

This story was created with love for every child learning to see themselves clearly and proudly.

Thank you to the parents, caregivers, teachers, and loved ones who encourage confidence, kindness, and self-love every day.

And to every child reading this—

♥ You are seen.

♥ You are valued.

♥ And you are loved,
just the way you are.

— Miss Betty Jewels

For all the kids who
Love their curls,
just the way they are.

Meet the Characters

Hi, I'm Miss Betty!

- As a hairdresser, I've always wanted to create a children's book that celebrates self-confidence, love, and embracing our hair!

- I believe that our kids need to see more representation like this.

- I'm so proud to be an author of books that uplift and inspire children to love themselves and their natural hair.

⭐ Meet Julia & Julian

Julia and Julian's names were inspired by " Jewels,",
from **Miss Betty Jewels**—because every child is a jewel.

- -

• I wanted to create characters that included both boys and
girls, especially in stories about hair, confidence, and self-love.
Too often, boys are left out of these conversations.

• Julia and Julian remind us that loving yourself, caring for your
hair, and feeling proud of who you are is for everyone.

Their story is about belonging, confidence, and growing
together.

Meet Julia!
Hi, I'm Julia!
I'm a fun-loving, confident little girl.
I love my curly, natural hair.
My favorite things are:
Playing dress-up
Painting and drawing
Playing with my brother Julian
Rainbows and flowers!

Meet Julian!
Hi, I'm Julian!
I'm a kind, curious, enthuciastic boy.
I love learning new things.
My favorite things are:
Playing soccer
Building things and solving puzzles
Going on adventures with my sister Julia.
Superheroes and video games!

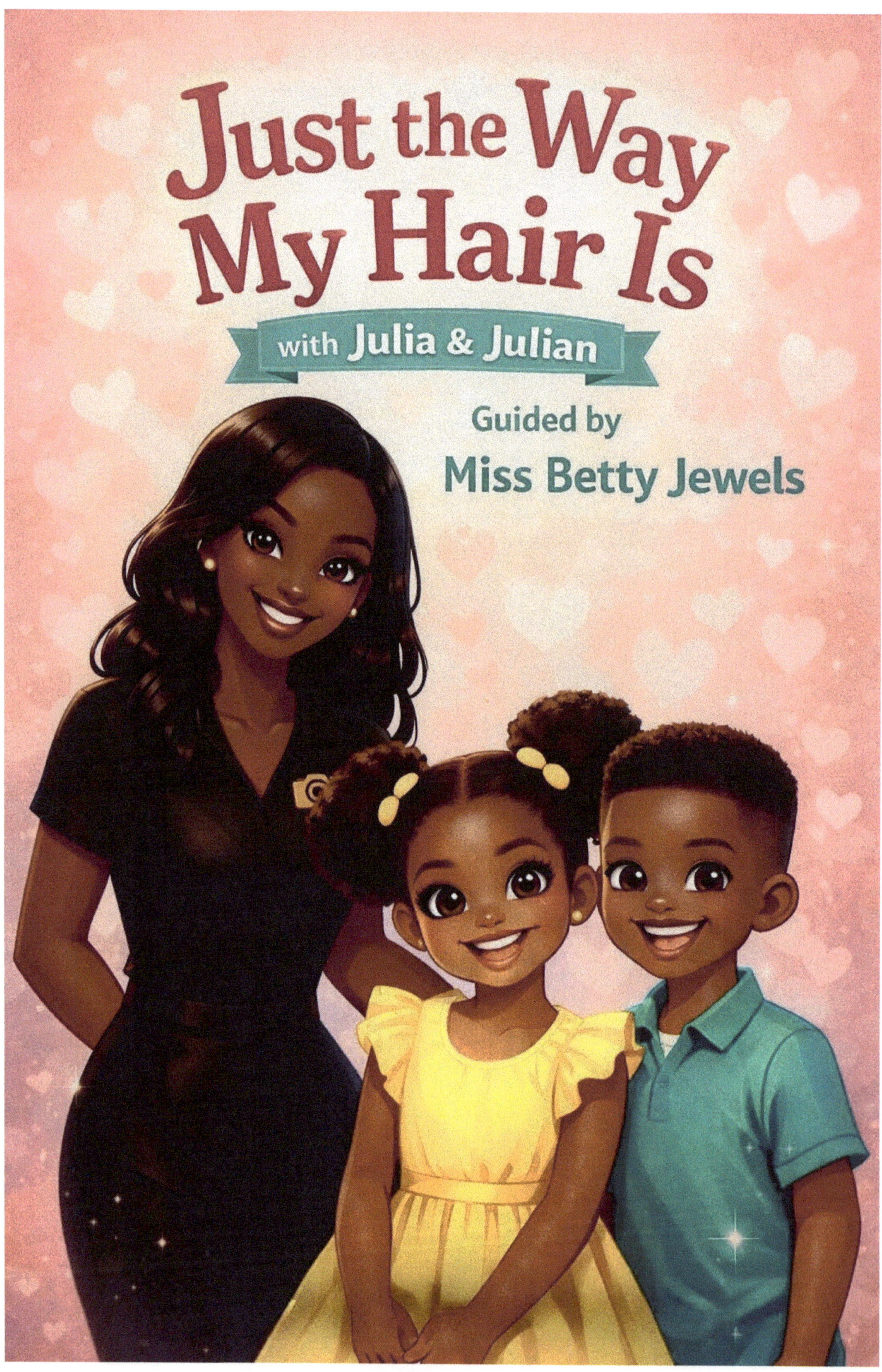

Just the Way My Hair Is
with Julia & Julian
Guided by
Miss Betty Jewels

Our Hair Is Special Because...

Our hair is special because it is **ours**.
It grows in its own way,
it feels different every day,
and it helps tell **our story**.

✦ Our hair can be:
   ✦ Curly
   ✦ Coily
   ✦ Puffy
   ✦ Soft
   ✦ Strong

And every kind of
hair is **beautiful**.

When we love our hair just the way it is,
we love **ourselves** too.

Julia loved her hair.

It bounced when she laughed and puffed up when she played.
Some days it felt soft, some days it felt wild —
but it was always **hers**.

Julian loved his hair too.

It curled and coiled right on his head,
never quite the same
two days in a row.
His hair followed him
everywhere he went.

They didn't rush to change it.
They didn't try to hide it.

They smiled...
because their hair was
already just right.

Some mornings, Julia looked in the mirror
and wondered what her hair would do today.
Would it stretch tall toward the sky
or curl up close like a cozy cloud?

Julian noticed his hair too.
After sleep, it sometimes
stood proud and playful,
other times calm neat.
No matter how it showed up,
it was always part of him.

Miss Betty smiled as she watched them.
She knew something important.

Hair isn't meant to *be perfect. it's **meant to loved.***

Sometimes Julia's hair needed extra care.
It liked water, gentle hands, and time to rest.
When her curls felt tired, she listened.
Her hair was telling her what it needed.

Julian learned to listen too.
Some mornings his coils stood tall,
other days they curled in close.
He smiled either way.

Their hair didn't have to look the same every day.
It just had to feel **loved**.

At school, Julia saw curls, coils, braids,
and puffs everywhere.
Some were tied up high.
Some were let loose and free.

Julian noticed it too.
Hair that stretched toward the sky.
Hair that curled close and tight.
Hair that told stories without
saying a word.

Miss Betty smiled and said,
"Look around you.
No two crowns are the same."

Julia touched her puffs
and felt proud.
Julian ran his fingers
through his curls and grinned.

Sometimes people had things to say.

About curls. About coils. About puffs that reached the sky.

Julia listened... then looked at her reflection.

Julian listened... then touched his hair and smiled.

They remembered what Miss Betty always said—

"What grows from you is already enough."

Julia stood still for a moment.
She took a breath and looked at herself.

"My hair is mine," she whispered.
"It grows the way it's supposed to."

Julian ran his fingers through his curls.
He smiled and said quietly,

"My hair is strong. My hair is me."

They didn't need to be louder than
anyone else. They just needed to hear
themselves.

"My hair is already enough."

At recess, all the kids began to say how much they loved their various "crowns".
I love my puff!
I love my hair!
I love my waves!
I love my braids!
I love my curls!

They laughed together,
happy andfree.

On the swings, on the slide,
with their hair bouncing
wild and wonderful.

"I love my curls," said a child, sliding down.
"I love my coils," Julian said, swinging high.
Their friends cheered from below and joined in.

"I love my puff!"
"I love my waves!"
"I love my braids!"

Their hair danced
in the sunlight breeze,
joyful as they were.

After recess, Julia and Julian gave Miss Betty a warm hug. They thanked her for teaching them that loving their hair no matter how it is, is more than enough.

Miss Betty smiled kindly.
"Your hair is already enough," she said.
"Different is beautiful.
Andbeinguniqueisawesome."sheadded.

Miss Betty watched them go and whispered,

"Remember this, always—
Your hair is part of you.
Your story matters.
And you are already enough."

And with that,
Julia and Julian smiled into their next adventure.

When they came back from school, they both ran to the bathroom to look at themselves in the mirror and remembered what Miss Betty taught them.

Julia looked at her reflection.
Julian did too.
They smiledandsaidit together-
"I love my hair just the way it is."

Affirmations
I am enough.
Kind
Proud
Brave
Loved
Confident
Courageous
Smart
I matter.
I am strong.

We are beautiful.
We are smart.
We are loved.
We are enough.

I love my puff!
I love my curls!
I love my braids!
I love my waves!

My hair is beautiful.
just the way it is.
I love my hair
just the way it is.

My Reflection

Today I learned...

My hair makes me feel...

One thing I love about my hair is...

My hair is beautiful, just the way it is.

✦ My Gratitude ✦

Thank you, hair, for…

Today I am thankful for…

My hair helps me feel…

Thank you, hair. Thank you, me.

💛 Parent & Caregiver Guide

Activities & Reflection

1- Talk Together

- What does loving your hair mean to you?

- How do you feel on days your hair looks different?

2- Activity: Hair Appreciation

Invite your child to:
- Draw their hair
- Describe how it feels
- Name one thing they love about it

Journal Prompt

- Today my *hair made me feel...*

- One thing I love about myself is...

Caregiver Tip

Encourage open, positive conversations about hair, identity, and self-confidence.

Remind children that care looks different every day — and that's okay.

3 + 3 = 5
4, 2 = 3

Miss Betty
Shapes

 Teacher's Guide

Encouraging Hair Positivity in the Classroom

💬 Create an Inclusive Environment

- Use diverse hair books/toys/colors in the classroom
- Discuss where hair textures come from
- Avoid terms like "good hair"

✋ Facilitate Discussions

- Use open-ended questions to prompt reflection.
- Guide children to notice, name, and *honor their feelings about their hair*
- Reinforce messages of care and self-love

📖 Introduce the Story

- Invite open minds by asking: "What do you think this story might be about?"
- Define affirmations. Example: "Repeat after me. 'I am enough.'"

📋 Follow-Up Activity – Pal Notes

- Invite your students to write or draw positive notes about a classmate's hair
- Focus their praise on kindness, confidence, and care.
- All notes are positive and affirming.

✦ Quick Reminders for Teachers ✦

- Representation matters—be mindful of your language, examples, and décor.
- Encourage hair and identity exploration — no style is "unprofessional" here
- Lift up students who may feel marginal zed or unseen.

Hair Vocabulary

Hair Vocabulary

Straight

Wavy

Curly

Coily

💛 All hair types are beautiful.

Hair Vocabulary

Hair & Feelings

Confidence
believing in yourself

Pride
feeling happy about who you are

Patience
taking your time

Self-Love
caring for yourself

♡ My hair is part of me.

Hair Tools

Wide-Tooth Comb
Spray Bottle
Hair Pick
Rattail Comb
Satin Bonnet
Hair Dryer

Thank you for spending this moment with us.
We hope this story reminded you
to be gentle with yourself,
to listen to your hair,
and to love who you are—just the way you are.

Every curl, coil, puff, and crown tells a beautiful story.
And your story matters.

✦ *With love,*

✦ *Miss Betty, Julia & Julian* ✦

✦ See You in the Next Story! ✦

Julia, Julian, and Miss Betty will
be back soon with more stories to tell...

See you soon! 💛